THE ENERGY EQUATION

Patrick Holford

CW00457676

First published in 1988
by ION Press, a division of The Institute for Optimum
Nutrition
5 Jerdan Place, London SW6 1BE

© Patrick Holford 1988

Cover Design : QA
Illustrations: Christopher Quayle

All rights reserved. No part of this publication may be
reproduced, stored in a retrieval system, or transmitted, in
any form or by any means, electronic, mechanical,
photocopying, recording or otherwise, without the prior
written permission of the publishers.

ISBN 1 87097 601 0

Printed and bound in Great Britain by
Brier Press, High Wycombe, Bucks

CONTENTS

ABOUT THE AUTHOR

Patrick Holford started his career in the field of psychology where he researched ways of maximising mental energy. His research led him into the field of nutrition which has been his speciality since 1979. In 1984 he founded the Institute for Optimum Nutrition, an independent centre for the research and practice of nutrition, of which he is a co-director. His time is divided between teaching and training nutritionists, seeing clients, writing and researching.

He is author of many popular nutrition books including The Whole Health Manual, Elemental Health, Vitamin Vitality, The Metabolic Diet, The Better Pregnancy Diet and The Family Nutrition Workbook, and writes for a number of national magazines and newspapers. He is also a postgraduate researcher in nutrition, at the University of Surrey, specialising in trace element research.

He is married, with two children and lives in London.

O

CHAPTER ONE

WHY FEELING JUST "ALRIGHT" ISN'T ALRIGHT

ENERGY, or rather a lack of it, is probably the most commonly experienced sign of ill health. In a survey conducted by the Institute for Optimum Nutrition 158 people were asked to list their most frequently experienced health problems. No less than 58 per cent, 92 people, listed fatigue, constant tiredness, lassitude or lack of energy as top of the list.

Although hard to measure, it isn't hard to know when you're under par. It becomes harder to get out of bed in the morning. A full day's work leaves you shattered. Gone is that "zip" you used to feel. Both mind and body somehow slow down. There's no energy to get enthusiastic about anything. Know the feeling? Most people blame it on the kids, the job, the weather or just getting older. For some, their lives literally grind to a halt. With constant tiredness comes depression and irritability. One client, having been diagnosed as 'depressed', said "Wouldn't you be if you had so little energy you had been unable to work for five years?"

But even if you think your energy level is alright the chances are you're still short of your full potential. In the ION

Survey mentioned earlier 58 per cent reported low energy at the start of the trial. After six months on special nutrition programmes 79 per cent reported improved energy. So 21 per cent of people noticed a definite improvement in energy despite thinking their energy level was fine anyway! When I first put into practice the methods described in this book my energy level soared even though everyone thought I was already energetic. I needed less sleep, my memory and concentration improved and I felt physically fitter. I even lost 1 stone in weight (which I have never put back on) without seemingly eating any less.

THE ENERGY EPIDEMIC

We are, it seems, in the middle of an energy epidemic. The problem is so many people experience low levels of energy that this low level has become the norm. Few doctors take the symptom of fatigue too seriously, nor know what to do, provided you don't have iron deficiency aneamia or some specific disease. Much like doctors in the 1950's who used to ignore the symptoms of PMT, fatigue is not considered as a health problem. But a lack of energy is the first sign that all is not well.

Energy isn't something you're born with. Nor does it come out of the blue. Every single cell in your body makes it, day in, day out. The fuel is food, more specifically carbohydrates, found in grains, vegetables, fruits and all forms of sugar. Your fuel supply affects your energy. So does your body's ability to turn food into energy - your metabolism. Metabolism is itself controlled by minute nutrients - vitamins and minerals - that process of turning food into energy.

Sometimes, when your available energy is needed elsewhere in the body, for example when you're fighting a cold virus, you can feel low in mental and physical energy. A number of diseases demand extra production of energy, which is directed towards conquering the disease in question. At times of stress, whether mental, emotional or physical, more energy is again demanded. It is at these times that you are most likely to notice changes in your energy level.

EXHAUSTION - THE EARLY WARNING SIGNS
The first step to boosting your energy levels is to notice when they need a boost. If your energy level is low, but you're doing more than you usually do sooner or later you'll end up exhausted. Your body will become tense, your mind confused, your emotions up and down.

Hans Selye, one of the world's foremost stress researchers, noticed a pattern to stress and exhaustion. He observed that most people, when exposed to some stress factor, whether emotional or environmental, would initially react strongly. Consider, for example, your first cup of coffee or cigarette, or your first day at a new, demanding job. The next phase involved adaption. Getting used to the extra stresses at work or the effects of cigarettes. The final phase, which it is the purpose of this book to help you avoid, was exhaustion.

There's a lot more to exhaustion than those times when you just want to lie in, switch off and put your feet up. Many of today's most common diseases only occur when your body simply can't cope with the demands placed on it anymore. Stress-related diseases include arthritis, many forms of cancer, frequent infections including thrush or cystitis, irritable colon, indigestion, dermatitis, headaches and migraines, depression and anxiety, more extreme forms of mental illness, eczema, asthma, PMT, high blood pressure, eating disorders - the list is almost endless. But even before these diseases manifest there are usually little aches and pains that herald their beginning to the trained observer.

Think of all the health problems you have, both large and small and notice which ones get worse when you're tired and stressed. These are your early warning signals that should alert you to do something to recharge your batteries. The following

7

checklist also shows you how you are right now - and how you could be.

HIGH VITALITY - CHART YOUR COURSE
Have you reached your energy potential?

☐ Do you need more than 8 hours sleep a night?
☐ Are you rarely wide awake and rearing to go within 20 minutes of rising?
☐ Do you need something to get you going in the morning, like a coffee, tea or cigarette?
☐ Do you often feel drowsy or sleepy during the day, or after meals?
☐ Do you get dizzy or irritable if you haven't eaten for six hours?
☐ Do you sometimes feel as if you had a heavy weight on your shoulders?
☐ Do you avoid exercise because you haven't got the energy?
☐ Do you fall asleep in the early evening or need naps some days?
☐ Would you describe yourself as apathetic?
☐ Is your energy level less now than it used to be?
Score one point for each 'NO' answer.
IF YOU SCORE....
8-10 You're above average for vitality. You may be able to improve your energy level even further by following the recommendations in this book.
5-7 You're about average, with plenty of room for improvement. After all, who wants to be average? Check your diet, and try the supplements recommended on page 45.
0-4 You badly need a recharge. You are probably midly 'glucose intolerant' and would do well to avoid all sugar, coffee and other stimulants for a trial one month period, as well as following the diet and supplements recommended in this book.

Energy is all a question of balance. Some people are naturally more energetic than others and consequently can take on more before reaching exhaustion. Even if your diet is perfectly tailored to producing the maximum amount of energy you can still exhaust yourself by working too hard and having too many late nights. The secret is to maximise your energy level by following the dietary and lifestyle recommendations in this book, and then work up to your capacity, but not beyond. If you follow these recommendations you'll find your tolerance for stress will increase, you'll need less sleep, you'll become physically fit faster, and your mind will become more alert and your memory sharper. You may not notice these effects until three months have passed, but what you will notice within the first month is a boost to your energy levels.

REDUCING YOUR STRESS LEVELS
But if, with your new found energy, all you do is push yourself beyond new limits, you'll end up exhausted once more, but this time with no reserve to call on. Check your own stress levels by asking yourself these questions.

STRESS CHECK
- [ ] Do you feel guilty when relaxing?
- [ ] Do you have a persistent need for recognition or achievement?
- [ ] Are you unclear about your goals in life?
- [ ] Are you especially competitive?
- [ ] Do you work harder than most?
- [ ] Do you easily become angry?
- [ ] Do you often do two or three tasks simultaneously?
- [ ] Do you become impatient if people or things hold you up?
- [ ] Do you find it difficult to openly admit failure or defeat?

If you answer 'YES' five or more times the chances are you're already overstressed and will stay that way however much your energy improves. Set yourself some realistic goals to restore some sort of balance in your life. Here are a few suggestions. You'll need to alter them to suit your own lifestyle and capacity.

*Limit your working week to, at most, 10 hours a day, five days a week.

*Keep at least 1 day a week completely free of routine work.

*Make sure you use this time to cultivate a relaxing hobby, do something creative or take exercise.

*Avoid obvious pressures, such as taking on too many commitments.

*Learn to see when a problem is somebody else's responsibility, and refuse to take it on.

*If you have an emotional problem you cannot solve alone, seek advice.

*Concentrate on one task at a time, and focus all your attention on the present.

*Learn to say what's on your mind instead of suppressing it. You don't have to be aggressive - just state your point of view clearly.

*Listen to what other people have to say to you, and about you.

*Look long and hard at all the stresses in your life. Make a list of them.

Set out to find a positive attitude to things which can't be changed. If change is possible - take action. Don't let things wear you down.

The next chapter explains how to maximise your body's production of energy. This alone will give you more energy to deal with the stresses in your life.

CHAPTER TWO

HOW TO
MAKE ENERGY

W HAT you experience as energy, whether mental or physical, is the end result of a series of chemical reactions that takes place in every cell in your body. The process that turns food into energy is called *catabolism*. By a carefully controlled sequence of chemical reactions, food is broken down into its component parts, and these are combusted with oxygen, to make a unit of cellular energy called *ATP*, which in turn makes muscles work, nerve signals fire and brain cells function. Years ahead of man's primitive attempts to produce energy, this magical process happens inside every single cell and the only waste products are water and carbon dioxide. But first of all, the fuel has to be refined.

FOOD FOR FUEL
    Although we can make energy from protein, fat and carbohydrate, carbohydrate rich foods are the best kind of fuel. This is because when fat and protein are used to make energy there is a build up of toxic substances in the body. Carbohydrates are the only 'smokeless' fuel. Carbohydrates can

be divided into starches, (or complex carbohydrates) and sugars (or simple carbohydrates). Grains, lentils, beans and vegetables, especially potatoes all contain complex carbohydrates, while fruit, all forms of sugar, including honey, and some vegetables contain simple carbohydrates.

Our cells need the simplest unit of carbohydrate, glucose, as fuel. So the first job of the body is to turn all forms of carbohydrate into glucose. This is the end goal of digestion. Special glands in the mouth, pancreas and small intestines secrete enzymes that gradually breakdown down large carbohydrate molecules into simple sugars. The same thing happens if you boil any food for long enough. Try this out by tasting the sweetness in a piece of raw potato, compared to a boiled or baked potato. Also test the sweetness of a piece of bread, then chew it for a long time. It actually becomes sweeter as the enzymes in your mouth get to work.

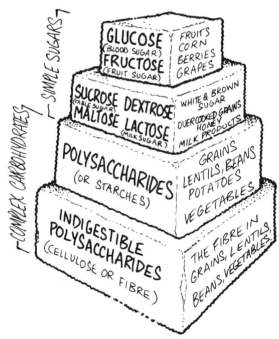

DIAGRAM 1 - The Sugar Family

All carbohydrate food is broken down into simple forms of sugar. The three simplest forms are *glucose, fructose* and *galactose*. All these can be absorbed into the bloodstream. Malt sugar derived from grains, is actually made out of two glucose molecules, known as *maltose*. Milk sugar is made out of a molecule of glucose and a molecule of galactose and is called *lactose*. What we know of as sugar, whether white or brown, is actually a combination of fructose and glucose, known as *sucrose*. Many fruits contain large amounts of fructose which requires no digestion at all.

If all you need is glucose you might think, as scientists did in the early part of this century, why not just eat sugar? By understanding what happens next you'll see why eating sugar can actually give you *less* energy.

BALANCING YOUR BLOOD SUGAR

Your bloodstream is your petrol tank. At all times it contains a relatively constant level of glucose. When your cells need energy they can call upon your glucose stores. But just in case blood sugar levels drop too much many cells, most notably muscle cells which use a lot of fuel, have their own reserve fuel, which is known as *glycogen*. The liver also carries a lot of glycogen. If you eat far more carbohydrates than you need, glucose and glycogen can be turned into a long-term storage form - fat. If really starved of fuel the body can breakdown protein in muscle tissue, for example, to use as fuel.

Consider the fate of a marathon runner, who, over 26 miles is going to burn a lot of fuel. As blood sugar levels drop, more and more glycogen, stored in muscles and in the liver, is converted to glucose. Once this runs out the runner must break down fat or protein to make energy. This is far less efficient and the pain and extra effort required is known as "hitting the wall".

The first key for maximum energy is keeping your blood sugar level constant. The best foods for doing this are complex

13

carbohydrates, because they break down gradually and release their sugar content slowly into the bloodstream. Fruit, which contains fructose, is also better than foods, like sugar, which rapidly break down to glucose and fructose. The reason for this is that fructose must first go to the liver where it is converted into glucose. This again slows down the increase in circulating glucose. So complex carbohydrates such as grains, beans, lentils, some vegetables, and also fruit because of its fructose content, are slow-releasing forms of sugar.

Sugar and most sweeteners including honey, malt, maple syrup, molasses and very refined foods, like most biscuits, cakes, white bread and cereals, whose processing and over-cooking has already turned their complex carbohydrates into simple sugars, are fast-releasing. Hardly requiring any digestion, they release their sugar content so rapidly into the bloodstream that they are akin to putting racing fuel into a mini. The blood sugar level rises rapidly, often giving a noticeable boost to energy, then the body races to lower blood sugar levels to avoid flooding, and blood sugar levels plummet, often too low, causing a drop in energy one to three hours after eating. This is called low blood sugar, or *hypoglycaemia* (hypo=low; glyc=sugar; aemia=in the blood).

Glucose levels in the blood are our short-term storage of fuel. The more even this supply, the better our cells can function. They are neither starved nor flooded with fuel and can call on reserves when needed. The blood sugar balance is carefully controlled by hormones, chemical messengers released from endocrine glands. *Insulin* from the pancreas helps lower blood sugar levels by helping to transport glucose from the blood into the cells. The manufacture of insulin depends upon vitamin B6 and zinc. Another hormone-like substance with a similar effect is *glucose tolerance factor (GTF)*. GTF is made in the liver. Its exact chemical structure is still a mystery even though it was first discovered in 1959. It contains vitamin B3, the mineral chromium and three amino acids.

14

FOODS THAT KEEP BLOOD SUGAR CONSTANT

Foods that elevate blood sugar levels rapidly have a high score, the highest being glucose. Foods with a low score are better 'energy foods'. Notice how foods containing fructose, or complex carbohydrates tend to have lower scores than refined foods.

FOOD	SCORE	FOOD	SCORE
SUGARS		**GRAINS**	
Glucose	100	White bread	69
Maltose	100	Brown bread	72
Sucrose	59	White spaghetti	50
Fructose	20	Brown spaghetti	42
Honey	87	White rice	72
Mars Bars	68	Brown rice	66
Lucozade	95	Sweetcorn	59
FRUIT		Buckwheat	51
Raisins	64	**BREAKFAST CEREALS**	
Bananas	62	Cornflakes	80
Orange juice	46	Weetabix	75
Oranges	40	Shredded wheat	67
Apples	39	Muesli	66
VEGETABLES		All-bran	52
Carrots (cooked)	92	Porridge oats	49
Potato (instant)	80	**BISCUITS**	
Potato (new)	70	Ryvita	69
Broad beans	79	Digestive	59
Peas	51	Rich tea	55
PULSES		Oatmeal	54
Baked beans	40	**DAIRY PRODUCTS**	
Butter beans	36	Ice cream	36
Kidney beans	29	Yoghurt	36
Chick peas	36	Milk (whole)	34
Lentils	29	Milk (skimmed)	32

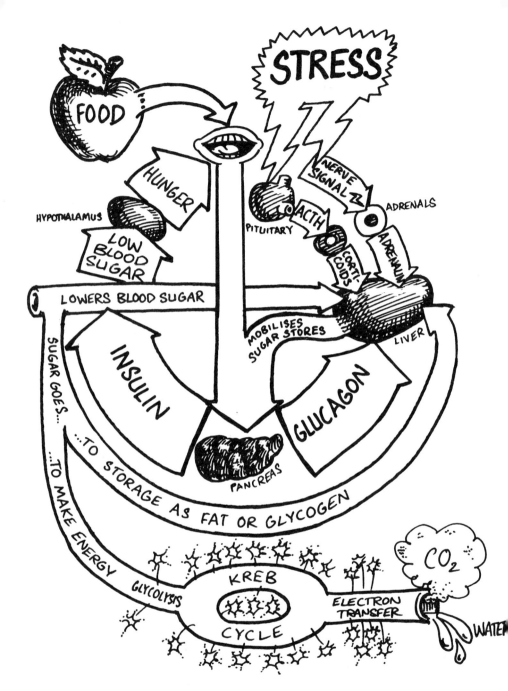

DIAGRAM 2 - The Sugar Cycle

Glucagon, another pancreatic hormone, can mobilise sugar stores in the muscles and liver if blood sugar levels get too low. An inability to produce insulin, or an inability to produce GTF results in elevated blood sugar levels in the blood. The cells become starved of glucose. This is diabetes, or hyperglyceamia (high blood sugar). Treatment is essential however nutritional therapy is often successful in, at least, reducing dependence on insulin.

BEATING THE SUGAR BLUES

Frequent eating of refined sugar and carbohydrates, such as biscuits, buns, cakes and sweets, upsets this delicate balance, often resulting in glucose intolerance, an inability to maintain even blood sugar levels. The symptoms are many and include fatigue, irritability, dizziness, insomnia, excessive sweating especially at night, poor concentration and forgetfulness, excessive thirst, depression and crying spells, digestive disturbances and blurred vision.

Although they do not contain sugar as such, stimulants like coffee, tea and chocolate have much the same effect as sugar because they stimulate the liver to release stores of glucose into the blood. Once more blood sugar levels rise, so does energy. But the effect is short-lived and in the long-term the regular use of such stimulants leads to lower and lower energy levels.

One client, Bobbie, serves as a case in point. She was already eating a healthy diet and took a sensible daily programme of vitamin and mineral supplements. She had only two problems: a lack of energy in the morning and occasional headaches - and one vice: three cups of coffee a day. After some persuasion she agreed to stop coffee for one month. To her surprise up went her energy level and the headaches stopped.

In the long-term, high levels of energy can only be sustained by avoiding refined carbohydrates and staying off stimulants. But these substances have a double sting. While they encourage the body cells to produce energy in the short-term they don't supply any of the vitamins, minerals or enzymes needed to turn sugar into energy. So frequent use of sugar and stimulants gradually depletes vital vitamins and minerals, especially chromium needed for the glucose tolerance factor. The refining of sugar, flour or rice loses over 90 per cent of the chromium content.

ARE YOU ADDICTED TO STRESS?

But if sugar and sweet foods are so bad for us, why do we like them so much? The answer to this simple question provides the answer to probably a third of all western diseases. The answer lies deeply rooted in our biological ancestry. Whether you like the idea or not, we human beings belong to the family 'primates' - that's monkeys and apes. Like our ancestors we are equipped with certain instincts, inborn programming for survival. One of these, the enjoyment of sweetness, is probably there to protect us from nature's more poisonous food. Almost anything sweet is safe. Fruits are safe, berries are safe. It's a good rule. For the plant kingdom it also makes sense, because when animals eat plants the seeds are deposited with a pile of manure - a good start in life!

But mankind, being smarter that its ancestors, learnt to extract and concentrate the source of sweetness until, in the 20th century, we are left with pure, white and deadly sucrose - sugar.

That's half the story. The other half is all about stress. All primates also have a powerful system for coping with stress. It's called the *fight-flight syndrome*, because it is designed to help you get up a tree if you're hunted, run faster if you're hunting and heal wounds rapidly if you're fighting. Even though today's stresses are more likely to be mortgages or demands at work, the same system operates. For example, if you're frustrated because you're stuck in a traffic jam your blood still coagulates faster, just in case you're wounded! Digestion also slows down to channel biological activity to increasing the supply of glucose to muscle cells for extra energy. We can't stop it happening - and the evidence suggests we don't want to stop stress even if we could.

Although we all complain about stress, could it be that there is a part of us that actually craves it? After all, given spare time, how many of us avoid stress? Instead we take part in or watch violent contact sports, drive around in fast cars, go skiing or do other such dangerous activities, and even if we do put our feet up, it's usually to watch the news, or the 2.5 murders that happen every night on our TV sets. Meanwhile, the children are playing space invaders or watching horror videos! Have you heard about Peter's Principle? It identifies that people like to get promoted in work to their level of incompetence! We strive for more pressure, more challenge. If we can't get it we turn to nutritional stressors like coffee, tea, chocolate, cigarettes or drugs. Consider the case of a rich housewife who repeatedly shoplifts. Such cases appear in the courts every year. Money isn't the motive. It's the thrill - the effects of the stress hormone, *adrenalin*.

We, like our ancestors, are addicted to adrenalin. But unlike our ancestors we don't fight, we don't hunt and we don't run. Our stresses no longer require a physical response. Yet for our ancestors and other primates it is the physical response that uses up the extra sugar that pours into our bloodstream. For us, we have to restore balance by producing more insulin, which lowers blood sugar levels by transporting the glucose into the cells, where it is converted to glycogen or fat. In fact, modern man produces gallons more insulin than his ancestors. With this context it is hardly surprising that diabetes, a disease in which the pancreas effectively stops producing insulin, is on the increase and accounts for 17% of all deaths.

Ultimately there is only one way out of the vicious circle of using adrenal stimulants to give you short bursts of energy. That is stop, or at least reduce, nutritional stressors. If, at the same time, you replace those nutrients that are used up by continual stress any 'withdrawal' effects are minimal and recovery to full vitality is fastest. The key nutrients mentioned so far are vitamin B3 and the mineral chromium, which are needed for glucose tolerance factor (GTF), and vitamin B6 and zinc, both needed in the production of insulin. But there are many more nutrients that are needed in the conversion of glucose into energy.

TURNING GLUCOSE INTO ENERGY

Within each of our thirty trillion or so cells exist tiny energy factories called *mitochondria*. The mitochondria turn glucose into another chemical, *pyruvic acid* , in the process of which a small amount of energy is released, which can be used by the cell to carry out its work. If this step occurs without sufficient oxygen present, a by-product builds up called *lactic acid*. That's why the first time you do strenuous exercise using muscles you didn't even know you had, the next day your muscles ache. This is, in part, because you've made them work too hard without supplying enough oxygen, causing a build up of lactic acid crystals. The more you exercise, develping larger muscles, the less strain you put on the muscles and the more oxygen they can use. This is what aerobic exercise is all about - providing muscles cells with enough oxygen so they can work properly.

Pyruvic acid then gets turned into *acetyl-coenzyme A*, or AcoA for short. This substance is perhaps the most vital because if you're starved of glucose, for example when a marathon runner "hits the wall", you can break down fat or protein to AcoA, and use this for energy. However it's rather inefficient so the body prefers to use carbohydrate for fuel.

From this point on oxygen is needed every step of the way. AcoA enters a series of chemical reactions known as the *Krebs cycle*, after its discover Ernst Krebs, which separates off hydrogen molecules, which then meet oxygen and BANG!

Energy is released. In fact over 90 per cent of all our energy is derived in this final stage. The waste products are carbon dioxide, which we exhale, water, which goes to form urine, and heat. That's why you get hot when exercising, because muscle cells make lots of energy, so heat is created.

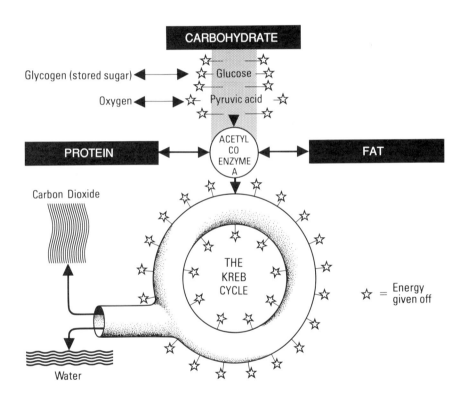

Reproduced from *The Metabolic Diet* with kind permission of Ebury Press.

DIAGRAM 3 - Turning Food into Energy

21

THE ENERGY NUTRIENTS

If you're thinking all you need to do is eat complex carbohydrates and keep breathing that's only half the story. All these chemical reactions are carefully controlled by enzymes, themselves dependent on no less than eight vitamins and five minerals. Any shortage of these critical catalysts and your energy factories, the mitochondria, go out of tune. The result is inefficient energy production, a loss of stamina, highs and lows - or just lows.

The important vitamins are the B complex vitamins, a family of eight different substances, every one essential for making energy. Glucose can't be turned into pyruvic acid without B1 and B3 (niacin). AcoA can't be formed without B1, B2, B3, and most important of all, B5 (pantothenic acid). The Krebs cycle needs B1, B2 and B3 to do its job properly. Fats and proteins can't be used to make energy without B6, B12, folic acid or biotin.

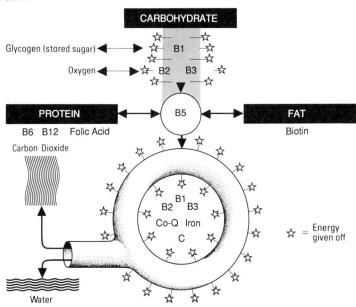

DIAGRAM 4 - Nutrients Needed to Turn Food into Energy

VITAMINS FOR VITALITY

It used to be thought that as long as you ate a reasonable diet you'd get enough B vitamins. But studies have shown that long-term slight deficiencies gradually result in a depletion of these vitamins in cells, causing early warning signs of deficiency such as poor skin condition, anxiety, depression, mental confusion, irritability, but most of all, fatigue. Many people's diets fall short on these vital vitamins. The Booker Survey in 1985 showed that only one in ten people ate a diet that provided the Recommended Daily Allowance for B6 or folic acid. In one study at the Institute for Optimum Nutrition a group of 82 volunteers, many of whom already had a "well balanced diet" were assessed to calculate their optimal nutritional needs. All 82 were given extra B vitamins in supplement form, often in doses twenty times that of the RDAs. After six months 79 per cent of participants reported a definite improvement in energy, 61 per cent felt physically fitter, and 60 per cent had noticed an improvement in their mental alertness and memory.

Being water soluble, B vitamins are easily lost when foods are boiled in water, as well as being extremely sensitive to heat. The best natural sources are therefore fresh fruit, raw vegetables, and wheatgerm. Seeds, nuts and wholegrains contain reasonable amounts, as do meat, fish, eggs and dairy produce. But these levels are reduced when the food is cooked or stored for a long time.

The minerals iron, calcium, magnesium, chromium and zinc are also vital for making energy. Calcium and magnesium are perhaps the most important because all muscle cells need an adequate supply of these to be able to contract and relax. A shortage of magnesium, so common in those who don't eat much fruit or vegetables, often results in muscle cramps, as the muscle in unable to relax.

But vitamins and minerals aren't all that's involved. The final stage before energy can be derived by reacting hydrogen with oxygen is dependent on a special coenzyme, coenzyme Q (Co-Q). A vital link in the chain, Co-Q provides the spark, together with oxygen, to keep our energy furnace burning.

The recent discovery that Co-Q is present in foods, that levels decline with age, and that cellular levels rise when supplements are taken, has led many nutritional scientists to suspect that Co-Q may be the missing link in the energy equation. The next chapter explains why and reviews the astonishing results that have been achieved through supplementation of this nutrient.

CHAPTER THREE

COENZYME-Q
THE MISSING LINK
IN THE ENERGY EQUATION

A new nutrient, Coenzyme Q, is showing miracle properties in helping patients with heart disease and other diseases in which energy production within cells is impaired. So astonishing are the properties of this nutrient that no less than 12 million people in Japan supplement their diets with Co-Q. In Kiev, in Russia, a research institute has been set up just to study the effects of this astonishing nutrient.

Co-Q was first isolated thirty years ago in Britain by a group of scientists working in Liverpool, and was identified as a critical component in the production of energy within cells. The recent discovery that Co-Q is present in foods, that levels decline with age, and that cellular levels rise when supplements are taken has led many scientists to consider Co-Q as an undiscovered vitamin. Technically, Co-Q cannot be classified as a vitamin since it can be made by the body even if it isn't made in large enough amounts for optimum health and energy. It is therefore a semi-essential nutrient.

Co-Q's magical properties lie in its ability to improve the cell's ability to use oxygen. In the final part of catabolism, when hydrogen is released during the Krebs cycle to react with oxygen, the actual reaction occurs at an atomic level, with the components of these elements, called*electrons*, being passed from one atom to the next. It's called the *electron transfer pathway*. These electrons, which are tiny charged particles, are highly reactive and need to be very carefully handled. They are like nuclear fuel - a very potent, but a very dangerous energy source.

So dangerous are these spare electrons that they are thought to be the initiating factor that makes some cells become cancerous, and makes cells within artery walls accumulate fats and cholesterol, heralding the beginning of heart disease. The damage caused to healthy cells by these spare electrons is a large part of what ageing is all about. The more damaged cells we have the biochemically older we are. Compounds that contain spare electrons are called *free radicals*. They are created both during catabolism, but also from smoking, eating fried food, breathing in pollution, and from radiation from the sun,

Co-Q has two key roles to play in handling these volatile electrons. It controls the flow of oxygen, making the production of energy most efficient, and prevents damage caused by spare electrons.

According to Dr Folkers, director of the Institute for Biomedical Research at Austin University, once body levels of Co-Q drop below 25% of normal, disease may ensue. His latest research, as yet unpublished, indicates that the ability to extract sufficient Co-Q from food declines with age, and may "turn off" altogether at some point. "The next puzzle is discovering why this happens - and when."

In the last decade well over a hundred research trials have been conducted in the USA and Japan with some astonishing results. Since Co-Q has such a critical part to play in the energy production of every single cell its use in promoting health is far reaching and perhaps best illustrated by recent trials on heart disease patients.

CO-Q SAVES LIVES IN HEART PATIENTS

In a six year study at the University of Texas involving people with congestive heart failure, a condition which the heart, the largest muscle in the human body, becomes progressively weaker, 75 per cent of those on Co-Q survived three years, compared to 25 per cent on conventional medication. In no less than twenty properly controlled studies published in the last two years Co-Q has, repeatedly demonstrated a remarkable ability to improve heart function and has now become the treatment of choice in Japan.

In a combined trial by the University of Austin, Texas and the Centre for Adult Diseases in Osaka, Japan, 52 patients with high blood pressure were treated either with Co-Q or dummy tablets. There was an 11% decrease in blood pressure for those on Co-Q, compared to a 2% decrease for those on dummy tablets.

Angina is a common condition in which sufferers experience pain in the heart region on exertion. It is usually caused by blockages in the tiny arteries that feed the heart muscle cells with oxygen. Since Co-Q helps all muscle cells to become most efficient this magical nutrient has also been investigated as a natural treatment for angina. In one study at Hamamatsu University angina patients treated with Co-Q were able to increase their tolerance to exercise and had less frequent angina attacks. After only four weeks on Co-Q other medication had effectively been halved.

CO-Q AND ATHLETIC PERFORMANCE

In a number of studies Co-Q has been shown to improve exercise tolerance by helping muscle cells use oxygen, and is likely to be of use to all people, especially athletes, wishing to maximise their physical performance.

With Co-Q supplements some angina patients have been able to double the time they can endure in exercise treadmill tests, but does this improvement occur in people without heart disease? A team of scientists from the Free University of Brussels decided to test the effects people. The study involved no exercise, just the addition of a daily 60mg Co-Q supplement for four to eight weeks.

After only four weeks significant improvement in heart function became evident. This improvement continued up to about eight weeks and then appeared to level off. Not only did maximum endurance improve, (a fact which is of litle significance to a sedentary person who is unlikely to exercise to the point of maximum endurance) but also the heart function, measured by its contractility, improved at the heart rate of 170 beats per minute, which is classified as a 'medium stress condition'. After four weeks contractility was up 12 per cent at this level, and up 28 per cent at maximum output.

Previous animal studies had shown clearly that fit animals have more Co-Q in their heart muscle tissue. Here was evidence that increasing Co-Q improved fitness *without exercise*. Although I would not wish to do anything other than encourage readers to keep fit by taking regular exercise, the evidence does suggest that Co-Q supplementation maintains a level of fitness in sedentary people without exercise and improves fitness in people who do exercise. Since the improvement levelled off, but did not decline, after eight weeks this suggests that once Co-Q levels reach a maximum within cells those cells can function most efficiently and will do so as long as Co-Q is supplemented. People on Co-Q, including myself, often notice that it becomes easier to maintain or build up to a level of fitness.

CO-Q BOOSTS THE IMMUNE SYSTEM

Since Co-Q helps control the build up of free radicals, dangerous forms of oxygen that are capable of damaging and destroying cells of the immune system, it is not surprising to find that Co-Q boosts the immune system.

COENZYME - Q

The immune system consists of special cells that recognise and destroy anything that is 'not us'. This could be an outside invader, like a virus or bacteria, or a body cell that has gone wrong, like a cancer cell. To test whether or not a nutrient boosts the immune system it is normal to measure production of these special immune cells, production of antibodies, which are tailor-made strait jackets designed to fit a particular virus, for example, themselves produced by immune cells, and to measure the success of the nutrient in increasing survival to viral diseases or cancer.

Working at the New England Institute, Dr Bliznakov, one of the first pioneers of Co-Q therapy, showed in 1968 that Co-Q supplementation more than doubled antibody formation on mice. Other studies have shown increases in other immune cells. He also showed that mice treated with a cancer producing substance were far less likely to develop tumours when given Co-Q. In one experiment 85 per cent of the control animals, not given Co-Q, developed tumours after 55 days, compared with 25 per cent given Co-Q. In studies in which animals were infected with specific viruses Co-Q has been shown to reverse the suppression of the immune system that occurs with some infections, and increase survival for fatal viruses. Needless to say, a potential role for Co-Q as part of a natural treatment for AIDS is now being investigated.

CO-Q EXTENDS HEALTHY LIFESPAN

Perhaps the most significant finding to come out of Dr Bliznakov's twenty years of research into Co-Q is its effect on ageing. Most scientists that the proper control of oxygen within cells is vital for increasing lifespan. It is also vital for increasing energy. Co-Q, it seems, does both. In animal studies, which for reasons of time have yet to be completed on humans, the lifespan of animals has been increased up to 50 per cent with Co-Q supplementation. One mouse reached the ripe old age of 150 weeks - equivalent to about 140 years in human terms!

THE ENERGY EQUATION

CO-Q IS SAFE AND EFFECTIVE

There is some disagreement as to whether Co-Q should be classified as a vitamin or just a semi-essential nutrient. Either way, no studies have reported toxicity even at extremely high doses taken over many years. There is no reason to assume that continued supplementation with Co-Q, as is advised for many vitamins, should have anything but extremely positive results.

Co-Q exists in many foods but not always in the form that we can make use of. There are many different types of Co-Q, called $Co-Q_1$ up to $Co-Q_{10}$. Yeast, for example, contains $Co-Q_6$ and $Co-Q_7$. Only $Co-Q_{10}$ is found in human tissues. It is this form of Co-Q that is effective in the ways described in this book and only this form should be supplemented. However, we can utilise 'lower' forms of Co-Q and convert them into $Co-Q_{10}$. This conversion process, which occurs in the liver, allows us to make use of Co-Q found in almost all foods.

But for some people, especially the elderly, the ability to convert lower forms of Co-Q into the active $Co-Q_{10}$ is impaired or non-existent. Exactly why and to what extent this occurs is not known. But for these people $Co-Q_{10}$ is an essential nutrient, a vitamin. It is likely to be for this reason that deficiency in Co-Q occurs.

Some foods contain relatively more $Co-Q_{10}$, and it is probably these foods that are our best dietary sources of Co-Q. These include all meat and fish, especially sardines, eggs, spinach, broccoli, alfalfa, potato, soya beans and soya oil, wheat, especially wheatgerm, ricebran, buckwheat, millet, and most beans, nuts and seeds.

Until recently these foods represented the only viable source of Co-Q. During the early days of research Co-Q was extracted, for experimental purposes, from beef heart, at a cost of £700 per gram. The human body contains about two grams. We need somewhere in the region of 10 and 60mg a day for optimum health. Until recently that would have cost £42 a day!

BEST FOOD SOURCES OF CO-ENZYME Q_{10} (Mg per Gm)			
FOOD	AMOUNT	FOOD	AMOUNT
MEAT		**BEANS**	
Beef	.031	Green beans	.0058
Pork	.024 to .041	Soya beans	.0029
Chicken	.021	Aduki beans	.0022
FISH		**NUTS & SEEDS**	
Sardine	.064	Peanuts	.027
Mackerel	.043	Sesame seeds	.023
Flat fish	.005	Walnuts	.019
GRAINS		**VEGETABLES**	
Rice bran	.0054	Spinach	.010
Rice	–	Broccoli	.008
Wheatgerm	.0035	Peppers	.003
Wheatflour	--	Carrots	.002
Millet	.0015	**OILS**	
Buckwheat	.0013	Soya oil	.092

In 1974 a Japanese company isolated a substance in the tobacco plant from which Co-Q could be produced. This provided more Co-Q for research but was still an expensive process. In 1977, again in Japan, a cheaper way of producing Co-Q through fermentation involving microorganisms, was discovered. Co-Q prices plummetted and supplements became viable.

Today many supplement companies offer Co-Q products. The best dosage is probably between 10 and 30mg a day. But do check they contain Co-Q_{10}, which is the active form of this nutrient.

THE ENERGY EQUATION

CHAPTER FOUR

THE ENERGY
EQUATION

THROUGH simple changes to your diet, backed up by basic supplementation of the key nutrients needed to turn food into energy, most people are able to improve their energy levels, sometimes way beyond their expectations. But improved nutrition doesn't work overnight. It usually takes one month to experience the first signs of extra energy. Almost everyone experiences more energy within three months. But the real long-term benefit only comes when your body has been optimally nourished for so long that new cells are made super-healthy. In seven years' time nearly every cell in your body will be new. A new you in seven years! In one year's time you will start to reap the long-term rewards, which go far beyond just extra energy.

But I am talking about real, consistent energy. The kind that gets you out of bed in the morning rearing to go, and gives you the stamina to maintain mental and physical energy throughout the day. Not some kind of hyped-up energy that comes from the short term effect of stimulants or stimulating situations.

YOU DON'T NEED STIMULANTS

Stimulants are energy's greatest enemy. Even though stimulants can create energy in the short-term, the long-term effect is always bad. So the first step to improving energy is to cut out, or cut down on stimulants. This includes coffee, tea, chocolate, sugar and refined foods, cigarettes, cola drinks and alcohol. It's worth knowing what each of these contain and what their effect is on the body.

Alcohol is made by the action of yeast on sugar. As such it has a similar effect as sugar. In the short term alcohol actually inhibits the release of reserve glucose from the liver and encourages low blood sugar levels causing an increase in appetite. The diseases associated with excess include diabetes, heart disease, cirrhosis and cancer of the liver.

Chocolate contains cocoa as its major 'active' ingredient. Cocoa provides significant quantities of the stimulant theobromine, whose action is similar to although not as strong as caffeine. Theobromine is also obtained in cocoa drinks, like hot chocolate.

Cigarettes contain nicotine, as well as sixteen other cancer producing chemicals. Nicotine is the primary stimulant and has a substantial effect even in small doses. In large amounts nicotine acts as a sedative. It is more addictive than heroin. People breaking the habit often experience low blood sugar problems.

Coffee contains theobromine, theophylline and caffeine, all of which are stimulants. Caffeine is the major stimulant, however decaffeinated coffee still contains the other two. Theophylline disturbs normal sleep patterns. Coffee consumption is associated with greater risk for cancer of the pancreas, and during pregnancy, increased incidence of birth defects.

Cola drinks can contain a quarter of the caffeine found in a weak cup of coffee. They usually contain sugar and colourings which also act as stimulants.

Medications provided for the relief of headaches may contain caffeine. Other caffeine tablets are available as stimulants. The most common are Pro Plus and the herb Guarana.

Tea contains caffeine, theobromine, theophylline and tannin. It is a stimulant and a diuretic with similar, although diminshed effects as coffee. A strong cup of tea can provide as much caffeine as a weak cup of coffee. Tannin interferes with the absorption of minerals. Tea drinkers have an increased risk of stomach ulcers.

REDUCING STIMULANTS WITHOUT SUFFERING

Of course, to cut all these out completely is not only just about impossible for many people, but is certainly stressful! The first step is to find out which of these are most important for you. First of all, look at your habits. Which of these, if any, do you have in one form or another several times a day? Which do you use as a pick-me-up, perhaps to get you out of bed in the morning or when your energy is flagging during the day? Which would you find hardest to stop completely for one month? When was the last time you went for one month without each of these stimulants?

Although you may intend to stop them for ever, in reality it is a lot easier to take one step at a time. So start by picking one stimulant (other than cigarettes) you use frequently. Could you realistically cut it out for one month only? If not, what could you reduce your intake to? Write this down and stick to it. Set yourself similar targets for no more than three stimulants. Sometimes they overlap. For example, if you use coffee, sugar and chocolate, but can't stand coffee without sugar, then cutting out sugar automatically means no chocolate and no coffee.

Here are some tips to help you get started.

SUGAR is an acquired taste. Although we are born with a liking for sweet things research has shown that only those who are fed sweets and sweet foods like high levels of sweetness. So as you gradually cut down the level of sweetness in all the food you eat you will soon get accustomed to this. That means having less sugar in hot drinks, less in food, even less dried fruit, and drinking more diluted fruit juice. When you want something sweet have fruit. Sweeten cereals and desserts with fruit, and if you're really desperate have a Sunflower Bar, or Take Off Bar (available from any health food shop) instead of chocolate or sweets. Don't substitute sugar with sugar substitutes. These may not raise your blood sugar levels, but nor do they allow you to change your habits. It takes one month to acquire the preference for less sweet foods. Let your taste buds be the judge of how sweet a food is - but do check the labels for all those disguised forms of sugar.

COFFEE is strongly addictive. It takes, on average, four days to break the habit. During these days you may experience headaches and grogginess. These are a strong reminder of how bad coffee really is for you. Decaffeinated coffee is only mildly better. The most liked coffee alternatives are Caro, Dandex and Symington's Dandelion coffee. When you have been off coffee for a month you may decide the occasional cup would be nice. Have this as a treat, perhaps when you eat out, not as a pick-me-up.

TEA is not as bad for you as coffee, unless you're the sort of person that likes your tea well stewed. Start by decreasing the strength of your tea, perhaps using a smaller cup or teapot. Tea has such a strong flavour that you can literally dip in a tea bag for seconds and still have a strong tasting drink. Use Luaka tea, which is a good quality Ceylon tea that is naturally low in tannin and caffeine. The most liked alternatives are Celestial Seasonings herb teas. Red Zinger and Mandarin Orange are my favourite. Red Bush (or Rooibosch) tea is good with milk.

CHOCOLATE contains sugar and chocolate. Start by having chocolate-free snacks, like Kalibu bars. Then switch to chocolate and sugar-free snacks like Take Off Bars or Sunflower Bars. Then avoid even these, keeping them strictly for emergencies, eating fruit instead when you want something sweet.

ALCOHOL is an easy habit to acquire because of its key role in social interaction. Start by limiting when you have alcohol. For example, don't drink at lunch-time. You'll certainly work better in the afternoon. Limit what you drink. For example, stick to wine, avoiding beer or spirits. Limit how much you drink by setting yourself a weekly target - for example, seven glasses of wine a week. This allows you to have quite a few at that party on Saturday night and compensate by having little throughout the proceeding week. Ideally, cut it out completely for at least the first two weeks. If you find this hard to do take a close look at your drinking habits, and, if necessary, seek professional help.

SMOKING can be one of the hardest habits to kick. The average smoker is not only addicted to nicotine, but is also addicted to smoking when tired, when hungry, when upset, on waking, after a meal, with a drink and so on. An excellent book that has helped many a hardened smoker stop is *How To Stop Smoking* by Simon Morgan (published by Virgin Books). Improved nutrition decreases craving for cigarettes so it's best to leave this one until you've been following the recommendations in this book for at least two months.

ENERGY OUT OF THE BLUE

One vital energy giving nutrient is oxygen. Without it there can be no energy at all. Exercise and breathing exercises all help to oxygenate the tissues and improve energy levels. The best forms of exercise are aerobic, stamina building exercises like swimming, jogging, exercise classes, cycling and brisk walking which all require you to breathe deeper and harder. With all forms of exercise deep breathing is beneficial. Time the movements with the breath and put your attention in the breath. Breathe from your stomach as this helps to open up the rib cage allowing more air in.

The breath is the link between mind and body. If you are stressed, angry or upset your breathing pattern will change. Just by concentrating on your breathing, making it as deep and slow as you feel comfortable with, helps to calm the emotions and clear the mind.

Start or end your day with at least ten minutes of stamina building exercise that really gets you breathing. It'll get you going in the morning and help you to relax and sleep at night.

THE HIGH VITALITY DIET

The key points to eating for vitality are:

Avoid refined sugars, including honey.

Avoid refined carbohydrates including white bread, biscuits, cakes, white rice and other junk foods.

Eat more beans, lentils and wholegrains.

Eat more vegetables, raw or lightly cooked.

Have four pieces of fresh (not dried) fruit a day.

Avoid coffee, tea, cigarettes and limit alcohol.

When you eat is as important as what you eat. Probably the most important meal of the day is breakfast. Many people skip breakfast or have a cup of coffee and a piece of toast. What you eat for breakfast determines how you feel for the rest of the morning. It is, however, also a mistake to eat so soon after surfacing that your digestive system is not yet fully functioning. If you start your day with ten or fifteen minutes of exercise your appetite will soon swing into action. Then it is time for a substantial breakfast, preferably containing some protein, but mainly complex carbohydrate foods or slow releasing sugars. Some ideas are given below in the *Seven Day Supercharge* menus.

What you eat during the day depends on your lifestyle. A diet high in fruit and vegetables is simply not as filling as our traditional diet high in fat and protein. This means you may need to snack on fruit mid-morning and mid-afternoon. If your day is stressful it is better to have a light lunch that requires little digestion, but most importantly, to get out of the office, put your feet up and stop thinking about work even if for only fifteen minutes.

You need at least two hours to complete the first stage of digesting a meal so dinner should never be later than two hours before the time you go to sleep. If you haven't quit all stimulants yet do avoid tea and coffee after 6pm.

SEVEN DAY SUPERCHARGE

Here are seven daily menus to help you get started and supercharged. By following these recipes for vitality, and taking the supplement programme recommended in the following pages you are likely to experience an improvement in your energy within a week. However the best is yet to come and well worth the effort.

Example daily menus are given first, followed by the recipes. You can make up your own menus by switching the individual breakfasts, lunches and dinners around. Each is well balanced in its own right.

DAY 1
Sesame and Banana Porridge

Cheddar Corn Salad & Wholemeal Bread

Chick Pea Feast with Spinach and Bean Salad
Baked Date & Apple

DAY 2
Apricot and Almond Yoghurt

Cottage Cheese and Alfalfa Sandwich & Coleslaw

Spaghetti Napolitana with Watercress Salad
Raspberry Sorbet

39

DAY 3

Apple Muesli

Baked Potato

Spicy Almond Couscous with Watercress Salad

DAY 4

Fruit Milkshake

Carrot Soup & Oat Cakes

Stuffed Peppers with Rainbow Root Salad
Apricot Whisk

DAY 5

Boiled Egg and Toast

Californian Gold Salad

Chestnut Hot Pot with Steamed Vegetables

DAY 6

Banana Yoghurt

Hummus & Crudite's

Fish Pie with Watercress Salad

DAY 7

Apple Muesli

Farmhouse Vegetable Soup & Wholemeal Bread

Kedgeree
Fruit Salad

RECIPES FOR VITALITY
BREAKFASTS

Sesame and Banana Porridge - Make porridge with half water, half skimmed milk and two dessrt spoons of ground sesame seeds. Serve with sliced banana and yoghurt.

Apricot and Almond Yoghurt - Soak unsulphured apricots and almonds overnight. Mix with plain yoghurt.

Banana Yoghurt - Chop a banana into plain, unsweetened yoghurt. Mix in wheatgerm, sunflower seeds, coconut flakes or ground sesame seeds to taste.

Apple Muesli - Soak a good quality, sugar-free muesli overnight in skimmed milk. Serve with a grated apple.

Fruit Milkshake - Liquidize peaches, strawberries or bananas (or any fruit you care to try) with ground almonds, dessicated coconut and some ice. Add in milk and liquidize again.

LUNCHES & SALADS

Cheddar Corn Salad - Mix Cheddar cheese, iceberg lettuce, green pepper, alfalfa sprouts, kernels cut from corn-on-the-cobs and cherry tomato halves. Make a dressing from ground cashews, mayonnaise, yoghurt and skimmed milk. Add herbs to taste.

Coleslaw - Mix white or red cabbage, carrots, onions and raisins with a mayonnaise, low fat yoghurt and skimmed milk dressing.

Californian Gold Salad - Slice and arrange an apple, banana, nectarine, kiwi fruit and eight grapes. Sprinkle with lemon juice and top with cottage cheese and alfalfa sprouts.

Watercress Salad - Mix watercress, cucumber, lettuce, green pepper and alfalfa sprouts with a French dressing.

Spinach and Bean Salad - Carefully strip spinach leaves from the stalk and soak them in cold water. Rinse leaves, drain and pat dry. Chop coarsley and mix with minced onion and cooked red kidney (or other) beans available in tins. Serve with a French dressing or olive oil, lemon juice and bouillion powder dressing.

Rainbow Root Salad - Grate carrots, parsnips and raw beetroot and mix with chopped parsley. Make an Island dressing by liquidizing carrot, tomato, tofu, mayonnaise, ground almonds, Vecon, milk and grated nutmeg.

Carrot Soup - Liquidize raw carrots, ground almonds, skimmed milk (or yoghurt), a vegetable stock cube or Vecon, and mixed herbs to a thick soup consistency. Warm gently and serve adding a squeeze of orange juice.

Farmhouse Vegetable Soup - Saute or simmer a sliced onion in a little water. Add in carrots, celery, leeks, potatoes, courgettes, tomatoes or cauliflower. Add in Vecon or a vegetable stock cube and plenty of herbs. Cover and simmer until all vegetables are just soft. Liquidize before serving.

Hummus - Soak chick peas overnight, then simmer in fresh water for 45 minutes with a crushed garlic clove. Put chick peas, garlic, lemon juice, tahini, yoghurt and olive oil in a liquidizer, adding water if necessary. Add black pepper to taste.

DINNERS

Chick Pea Feast - Cook chick peas. Mix with chopped boiled eggs, flaked tuna fish and onion. Separately mix olive oil, vinegar, mustard, pepper, chopped parsley and chives and pour over chick peas. Serve hot.

Spaghetti Napolitana - For sauce, saute an onion, garlic, carrots, green pepper and mushrooms. Add tomato puree, thyme and vegetable stock. Simmer and serve with wholemeal spaghetti.

Spicy Almond Couscous - Saute an onion. Add in sliced carrots, red pepper, courgettes and mushrooms. Add tomatoes, pepper or chilli sauce, almonds, raisins and water. Simmer for 20 minutes. Meanwhile pour boiling water over couscous and leave for 15 minutes.

Stuffed Peppers - Cook green peppers in boiling water for five minutes. Cut off top and scrape out seeds. Fry onion, garlic and tomatoes until softened. Add rice, mushrooms, and stock. Simmer until cooked. Add egg, parsley and black pepper. Stuff

peppers and cook peppers in the oven.
Chestnut Hot Pot - Use fresh chestnuts or soak dried chestnuts overnight. Saute an onion. Add in parsnips, swede, potato, turnip, bouillon powder and herbs and simmer gently until chestnuts are cooked.
Fish Pie - Steam white fish, smoked haddock and prawns. Combine with bechamel sauce made with wholemeal flour. Add in mushrooms, herbs and pepper. Top with mashed potatoes and bake in oven for 30 minutes, sprinkling cheese on top.
Kedgeree - Mix boiled brown rice, colouring-free smoked haddock, chopped boiled egg, chopped parsley, paprika and pepper. Serve hot.

DESSERTS
Baked Date and Apple - Core cooking apples and stuff with dates. Sprinkle with cinnamon and bake in an oven until soft.
Raspberry Sorbet - Freeze whole raspberries and bananas (this can be done with any fruit). Allow them to thaw for five minutes, then liquidize and serve immediately.
Apricot Whisk - Stew dried apricots until soft. Liquidize with vanilla essence, yoghurt and curd cheese. Whisk egg whites stiffly and fold into mixture. Cool before serving.

SUPPLEMENTS FOR SUPERCHARGE
Many nutrients are needed to turn food into energy. These are Co-Q, vitamins B1, B2, B3, B5, B6, B12, folic acid, biotin, vitamin C, calcium, magnesium, iron, zinc and chromium. Not only is it wrong to assume that sufficient amounts of these are provided in the average diet, it is also wrong to assume that sufficient levels to produce your maximum potential for energy are provided in even the best of diets. The advice in this book aims to maximise the amount of nutrients you can get from diet and make up the shortfall through sensible, balanced use of nutritional supplements.

If you are sceptical about nutritional supplements you have nothing to lose except your scepticism by trying this supplement programme for one to three months. Nutrients in supplement form are neither dangerous nor toxic nor create 'dependencies'. They are simply concentrated food nutrients in pill form. Often the doses that produce results are many times higher than the levels found in food. Some people become unduly alarmed by this although there is no need to. A tenfold increase in dietary intake of most nutrients leads to no more than a doubling of available nutrient to the cells. So relatively large amounts need to be taken to saturate cells with these vital catalysts, so maximizing cell efficiency. What's more the body knows how to deal with excesses, perhaps with the exception of fat soluble vitamins A, D, E and K in very large quantities.

SUPPLEMENTS FOR SUPERCHARGE

NUTRIENT	BASIC LEVEL	HIGH ENERGY	SUPERCHARGE
Co-Q10	10mg	30mg	60mg
B1	25mg	50mg	75mg
B2	25mg	50mg	75mg
B3	50mg	100mg	150mg
B5	50mg	100mg	200mg
B6	50mg	75mg	125mg
B12	5mcg	10mcg	15mcg
Folic Acid	50mcg	100mcg	150mcg
Biotin	50mcg	100mcg	150mcg
Vitamin C	1,000mg	2,000mg	3,000mg
Calcium	150mg	300mg	450mg
Magnesium	100mg	200mg	300mg
Iron	10mg	15mg	15mg
Zinc	10mg	15mg	20mg
Chromium	20mcg	100mcg	200mcg

The chart on the previous page shows the ideal daily intake of each nutrient in supplement form, assuming your diet provides a little extra. The **basic** level is recommended for everybody to maintain a basic level of good health. The **high energy level** is for those wanting maximum energy or under a lot of stress. The **supercharge** level is the maximum one should take for up to one month to restore very low energy levels.

This long list of nutrients is best obtained by supplementing your diet with a high potency multivitamin and mineral, and an additional high potency B-complex, which contains all the B vitamins from B1 to biotin, together with a Co-Q supplement.

Many reputable companies produce high potency multivitamin and mineral supplements to match these doses, however only two at the time of writing produce Co-Q supplements. These are **Nature's Best**, and **Health+Plus**, both of whom have a mail order service (see Useful Addresses for their details). They also have other supplements that match these recommendations.

Supplements, being food nutrients, are best taken with food, preferably with breakfast or at lunchtime. The cost of such a programme is in the order of 40p a day - the price of a cup of coffee, a glass of wine, or six cigarettes. The benefits of taking these supplements, together with the dietary recommendations, is yours to experience.

COENZYME - Q

USEFUL ADDRESSES

HEALTH+PLUS Ltd supply vitamin and mineral supplements, including Co-Q, by mail order. Ring or write to Health+Plus Ltd, Health+Plus House, 118 Station Road, Chinnor, OXON OX9 4EZ Tel: 0844 52098.

THE INSTITUTE FOR OPTIMUM NUTRITION offers courses and personal consultations with trained nutritionists, including Patrick Holford. A directory of ION-trained nutritionists is available for £1. To receive ION's information pack please ring or write to ION, 5 Jerdan Place, London SW6 1BE Tel: 01 385 7984.

NATURE'S BEST Ltd supply vitamin and mineral supplements, including Co-Q, by mail order. Ring or write to Nature's Best Ltd, PO Box 1, Tunbridge Wells KENT TN2 3EQ Tel: 0892 34143.

RECOMMENDED READING

The following books will help you dig deeper into nutrition and energy.

Patrick Holford - *Vitamin Vitality* (ION Press) 1985. A thoroughly researched book which establishes why so many people are sub-optimally nourished and how to work out your own vitamin and mineral needs for optimum health.

Patrick Holford - *The Metabolic Diet* (Ebury Press) 1987. This book explains how to boost your metabolic rate and lose weight permanently. As well as explaining the 'mechanics' of weight control, this book is highly practical with a 30 day diet and delicious recipes.

HOW TO BOOST YOUR IMMUNE SYSTEM
by Jennifer Meek

The first in the *Nutrition Connection* series, this book explains how the immune system works and what you can do to make yours healthy. It include the Immune Power Diet, an action plan for immune strength. (£1.99)
ISBN 1-870976-00-2

VITAMIN VITALITY
by Patrick Holford

Are you getting all the vitamins you need, even in a well-balanced diet? Patrick Holford thinks not. He presents convincing evidence that 80 per cent of people don't even get the minimum recommended levels.

In this topical - and, at times, controversial - book shows how, with a careful intake of vitamins and minerals, both from your diet and from supplements, you can achieve optimum health and get the very best out of yourself. (£3.95)
ISBN 0-00-411979-7

These books can be ordered from any bookshop, or, in case of difficulty, post-free direct from ION Press, 5 Jerdan Place, London SW6 1BE.